IMAGES
of America

CLEVELAND
1796–1929

For my wonderful daughter, Thealexa.

IMAGES
of America

CLEVELAND
1796–1929

Thea Gallo Becker

ARCADIA
PUBLISHING

Published by Arcadia Publishing
Charleston, South Carolina

Library of Congress Catalog Card Number: 2004102270

For all general information contact Arcadia Publishing at:
Telephone 843-853-2070
Fax 843-853-0044
E-mail sales@arcadiapublishing.com
For customer service and orders:
Toll-Free 1-888-313-2665

Visit us on the Internet at www.arcadiapublishing.com

CONTENTS

ACKNOWLEDGMENTS

The photographs used in this book were obtained entirely from Cleveland State University Library's Special Collections, William C. Barrow, Special Collections Librarian. I appreciate all the help and support provided by the staff, who allowed me to select the best images to represent the areas I wished to highlight. The CSU Special Collections area is an outstanding repository of photographs and newspaper clippings from *The Cleveland Press*. Many of these outstanding images may be found on their Cleveland Memory Web site: http://web.ulib.csuohio.edu/SpecColl/.

There are many books available on Cleveland's history. I found the following to be the most comprehensive and useful: *Cleveland: The Making of a City*, by William Ganson Rose, 1950; *Yesterday's Cleveland*, by George E. Condon, 1976; *The Encyclopedia of Cleveland History*, edited by David Van Tassel and John J. Grabowski, 1987; *Cleveland: A Concise History, 1796:1990*, by Carol Poh Miller and Robert Wheeler, 1990; *Landmark Architecture of Cleveland*, by Mary-Peale Schofield., 1976; *Cleveland Architecture: 1876-1976*, by Eric Johannesen, 1979; and *Trolley Trails Through Greater Cleveland and Northern Ohio*, by Harry Christiansen, 1975.

INTRODUCTION

The city of Cleveland was founded in 1796 by General Moses Cleaveland, who led a surveying party to the Western Reserve as an agent of the Connecticut Land Company. (The "a" in Cleaveland was later dropped.) Located on the southern shores of Lake Erie in northeastern Ohio, Cleveland developed from a modest frontier settlement of a few dozen homes into a bustling center of commercial activity for all of Cuyahoga County. In 1815, Cleveland became a village, and by 1824, with a population nearing 500, Cleveland was a successful port of entry due to its lakefront border and location at the northern mouth of the Cuyahoga River. When Cleveland was incorporated as a city in 1836, the population exceeded 5,000. Cleveland had a New England-style Public Square, which would become the heart of its downtown area, and the first streets, Superior and Ontario, attracted wealthy, influential settlers, and their businesses.

The low-lying area flanking both the east and west banks of the Cuyahoga River would become known as the Flats. It would be this area that would help transform Cleveland into a manufacturing and industrial giant in the second half of the 19th century. John D. Rockefeller, who came to Cleveland in 1853, founded the Standard Oil Company and became the nation's first billionaire. The Flats had developed into the industrial center of Cleveland, which in turn became the manufacturing and industrial center for the Northern Ohio region. The arrival of Irish, German, and Italian immigrants as laborers and skilled artisans and craftsmen, together with the developing railroad industry, helped push Cleveland's population to nearly 44,000 by 1860. At the end of the Civil War, Cleveland's population surpassed 90,000, and its iron and steel industries flourished during this industrial age.

In 1890, the Arcade, the nation's first indoor shopping center, opened to the public. A building boom seized Cleveland as historic landmarks such as the Cuyahoga Building, the Williamson Building, and the Soldiers and Sailors Monument further defined downtown Cleveland. Euclid Avenue was dubbed "Millionaires' Row," as it was lined with stately mansions belonging to Cleveland's industrial, commercial, and political elite such as Tom L. Johnson, streetcar magnate and arguably Cleveland's finest and most progressive mayor. When Cleveland celebrated its centennial in 1896, it had a population well over a quarter million. At the turn of the century, Cleveland had become the sixth largest city in the nation.

During the first two decades of the 20th century, Cleveland pursued two ambitious development projects that would change the character of Public Square and the lakefront's landscape. The Group Plan for civic renovation would transform the mall area near the lakefront with the addition of several classical-style government buildings, including a new City Hall, the Cuyahoga County Courthouse, and a Federal Building. In 1923, ground was formally broken for the Cleveland Union Terminal and Terminal Tower project on the south side of Public Square, realizing the dream of brothers O.P. and M.J. Van Sweringen. The

Terminal Tower would become Cleveland's newest, most recognizable landmark at a time when the population was nearing one million.

Cleveland is a city with many cultural treasures. University Circle, located on Euclid Avenue at East 105th Street, is home to the Cleveland Museum of Art, founded in 1916, and the Cleveland Orchestra, founded in 1918 as one of the finest orchestras in the world. The Cleveland Play House Square District on East 14th and Euclid Avenue gave the city a dynamic theater life, attracting nothing but the finest entertainment.

While searching through vintage photographs, particularly those featuring Public Square, I was impressed at Cleveland's ability to use its many resources, be they commercial, industrial, social, or even cultural, to create a model other cities aspired to imitate. Cleveland was a city of many firsts, with a pool of talent that served not just our community, but others as well. Perhaps Cleveland will find that greatness one day again.

–Thea Gallo Becker

NATIVE AMERICAN CELEBRATION. In 1896, centennial celebrations highlighted Cleveland's summer season. Here, a family of Native Americans wear traditional dress and stand beside a teepee on the northwest corner of Public Square. Directly behind the assembly is the Old Stone Church, a historic landmark.

8

One

CLEVELAND'S EARLY
YEARS

CENTENNIAL LOG CABIN. Major Lorenzo Carter was the first permanent settler of Cleveland. Major Carter came to the area in 1797, building a log cabin on the east bank of the Cuyahoga River. This cabin was built to resemble pioneer architecture and was placed on the northeast corner of Public Square. It was dedicated at a centennial celebration on July 21, 1896, sponsored by the Women of the Early Settlers Association. The sign next to the door reads, "Centennial Log Cabin Tavern."

The Ohio and Erie Canal. The significance of the Ohio and Erie Canal in the development of Cleveland, Cuyahoga County, and all northeast Ohio cannot be underestimated. Alfred Kelley, one of the most influential of Cleveland's early settlers, pushed for the northern terminal of the canal to be located at the mouth of the Cuyahoga River as it flowed into Lake Erie. This photograph was taken near the five-mile lock, *c.* 1890.

Building the Canal. The path of the Ohio and Erie Canal followed the Ohio River from Cleveland down to Portsmouth, Ohio. Canal construction began in 1825 when Cleveland was a village of 500 and was completed in 1832. Cleveland's economy grew strong as trade with merchants from Lake Erie sealed the city's reputation as the commercial heart of Cuyahoga County. This photograph was taken near the 12-mile lock, *c.* 1900.

OLD TRINITY CHURCH. The first church to be built in Cleveland was called Trinity Church and was originally located on the southeast corner of St. Clair Avenue and West 3rd Street. The Episcopalian parish of Trinity Church was incorporated in 1828, and in August of 1829, the church was open for worship. Trinity Church was a simple, white wooden-framed structure with a central tower.

CLEVELAND'S NEW ENGLAND CHARACTER. Early drawings of Cleveland's beginnings show a town planned according to the New England roots of its founder, General Moses Cleaveland, featuring a central meeting place or Public Square filled with many trees. In 1836, Cleveland was officially designated a city with a population surpassing 5,000. The view here looks east from West 6th (formerly Bank) Street and St. Clair Avenue. Trinity Church, Cleveland's first house of worship, is in the center.

COMMODORE PERRY AT PUBLIC SQUARE. Commodore Oliver Hazard Perry's victory in the Battle of Lake Erie was commemorated with a sculpture of the hero by William Walcutt, dedicated in 1860, and placed in the center of Public Square on Superior Avenue. This was Cleveland's first public monument. In the right background, the tall spire of the landmark Second Presbyterian Church is visible behind Public Square's many beautiful shade trees.

VIEW FROM WEDDELL. Peter M. Weddell was an early settler and businessman who built Cleveland's first luxury hotel, the Weddell House, in 1847 on the corner of Superior Avenue and West 6th Street. This view taken c. 1876 provides a glimpse of the city as seen from the five-story Weddell. Standing tall behind the City Hotel is the Old Stone Church, an early Cleveland landmark that remains on Public Square.

FENCING IN PUBLIC SQUARE, 1857. As Cleveland grew in population and size, resentment stirred between those desiring preservation of the residential and park-like character of Public Square and those viewing the area as the ideal center for commercial activity. Superior Avenue and Ontario Avenue were the first city streets, and merchants thought they should run through Public Square. Opponents who wanted the roads to stop at Public Square erected fences to block traffic coming from Superior and Ontario Avenues. The fence is visible in the center at left as a public fountain pumps water in from Lake Erie. The fence remained an issue for 10 years until it was removed, and all of Public Square was opened. Looking east on Superior Avenue, a thriving commercial block is seen on the right, anchored on the southwest corner of Superior and Public Square by the Forest City House, established in 1851 and one of Cleveland's earliest and grandest hotels. This location would remain prime space for hotels up through the present day.

THE LEMEN HOMESTEAD. William Lemen was an early settler and a businessman who traded in many basic commodities. He is remembered for the home depicted in this *c.* 1830 drawing that faced Public Square on the south side of Superior Avenue, then one of the major residential and upcoming commercial streets of Cleveland. It was the first house built on Superior south and one of the few homes built of stone. It was razed in 1854.

HOFFMAN'S BLOCK. One of the earliest commercial blocks was built *c.* 1855 on the former site of the Lemen homestead. Entrepreneur E.B. Hoffman erected the four-story brick building on Superior Avenue, facing the east side of Public Square, to lease office and retail space. Hoffman's Block is the first structure on the right side behind the shade trees. Cleveland's abundance of trees in and around Public Square earned it the nickname "Forest City."

THE OLD FEDERAL BUILDING. Located on Superior Avenue across the street from Hoffman's Block, the original Federal Building was erected in 1858 on a parcel of property belonging to Leonard Case Sr., an early prominent settler who helped shape Cleveland's business, civic, and cultural base. This building was designed in the streamlined classical style prevalent for this time period. It was razed in 1902.

THE CASE COMMERCIAL BLOCK. The Case Block was built in 1875 by philanthropist Leonard Case Jr. (1820–1880), son of Leonard Sr., an early and prominent settler of Cleveland. Located at the intersection of Superior Avenue and Wood Street, the Case Block included office and retail space and provided temporary quarters for City Hall. The building was razed in 1921 for construction of the Public Library.

DEMONSTRATION ON PUBLIC SQUARE. Clevelanders became increasingly aware of fire hazards and welcomed innovations to protect the city and its population. In 1869, the first demonstration of the city's first fire engine testing its fire hose drew record crowds on Public Square. The city's fire department was organized in 1834. The Forest City House is seen on the right, and the Perry Monument is seen in the left background.

THE BANDSTAND ON PUBLIC SQUARE. Cleveland's Bandstand, an open wooden-framed pavilion set on a raised platform surrounded by shade trees, was located on the northeast corner of Public Square. At the time, Public Square was officially known as Monumental Park in recognition of the Commodore Perry Monument. Concerts were often given, particularly during summertime, which added to Public Square's appeal as a popular place of recreation.

THE ARCH OF TRIUMPH. European immigration was pivotal to the development of Cleveland. The German population, one of the earliest ethnic groups to help build and influence the city, celebrates the end of the Franco-Prussian War in 1871 with a three-day event centered around this arch erected behind the Perry Monument on Public Square. The success of the Peace Jubilee underscored the rise and importance of the German community.

THE SPIRIT OF 1876. The 4th of July celebration was particularly exciting in 1876 when Clevelanders were treated to a hot-air balloon exhibition. Thousands of spectators filled Public Square to witness the very first flight of its kind demonstrated in Cleveland. Positioned behind the Perry Monument, the "Buffalo" balloon is just moments away from its historic ascent.

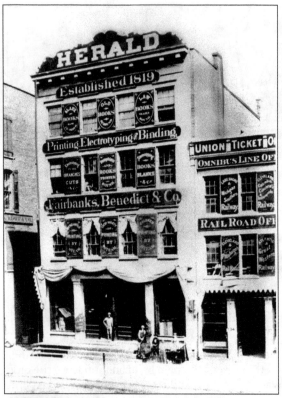

THE HERALD. Cleveland's oldest newspaper, *The Herald* was established in 1819 by Eber D. Howe four years after Cleveland was incorporated as a village. The Herald Building, as seen in this 1873 photograph at its location on Bank Street, became the first business block in the city to have a façade made completely of stone instead of the typical frame fronts. *The Herald* newspaper ended publication in 1885.

SUPERIOR AVENUE. Prior to 1852, Superior Avenue was known as Superior Street. The commercial growth of the area cemented Superior's status as Cleveland's business center, and it was renamed an avenue. In this early 1880s photograph, the view is looking north with the Weddell House at left and the Merchants National Bank at right. As seen at right, the electric light and telephone poles stood high and had five cross-arms.

THE FOUNTAIN ON PUBLIC SQUARE.
Located on Public Square was an attractive, circular fountain surrounded by an iron fence. In this photograph c. 1870, the fountain is set against a backdrop of Superior Avenue's busy commercial block. The building at the far right houses Cleveland's City Hall and other city offices. City Hall had always occupied rented quarters and would continue to do so until 1916 when a new City Hall would be bulit on Lakeside Avenue.

POLICE BEAT ON SUPERIOR AVENUE.
Police in 1874 were bearded, as shown by the two officers standing on the north side of Superior Avenue near West 3rd (formerly Seneca) Street in the heart of the city's business district. Pictured here is a commercial strip of brick and stone buildings often with offices on the upper floors and retail shops at ground level. J.M. Copeland and Company Photographic Gallery is seen in the center of the block.

THE CANNON ON PUBLIC SQUARE. The monument commemorating the success of Commodore Oliver Hazard Perry was not the only tribute to the heroes who defeated the British in 1813. Located on the northeast corner of Public Square, a cannon captured in the historic Battle of Lake Erie stood proudly for years. The inscription read: "Thirty-six pounder surrendered by Captain Robert Barclay to Commodore Perry in the Battle of Lake Erie."

THE SOCIETY FOR SAVINGS BUILDING. The first Society for Savings banking establishment, as seen in this 1869 photograph, was built on the northeast corner of Public Square on Rockwell Street in 1867. Architect Joseph Ireland used red brick and stone to highlight his impressive high Gothic design. The Society for Savings Building was significant as it was the first fireproof building erected in Cleveland.

THE NEW SOCIETY FOR SAVING BUILDING. Across the street from the Old Stone Church, construction is underway for the new Society for Savings Bank Building, erected during 1889–1890. John Wellborn Root designed the building, and it was built on the site of the former residence and commercial block of successful jeweler Newton E. Crittenden. Notice that the Old Stone Church is still topped by a 250-foot steeple.

PUBLIC SQUARE NORTHWEST. In 1900, the Old Court House (at left) was an imposing brick building that stood on the northwest corner of Public Square next to the Lyceum Theater, which opened in 1889. Next to the theater, on the right, was the historic First Presbyterian Church of Cleveland, commonly referred to as the Old Stone Church since it was the first Cleveland church built entirely of stone. The massive steeple is now gone, a casualty of fire.

CLEVELAND AND THE CIVIL WAR. In 1865, hundreds of Civil War veterans pose for this photograph taken on Public Square. Clevelanders supported the call to arms by President Abraham Lincoln and sent thousands of citizens, young and old, to fill the Union ranks. They were memorialized by the Soldiers and Sailors Monument, which replaced the figure of Commodore Perry as Cleveland's landmark.

REMEMBERING LINCOLN. Cleveland was privileged to be one of the rail stops as the body of President Abraham Lincoln was moved and the nation paid its final respects. A pavilion was erected on Public Square to shelter the catafalque upon which the coffin bearing the slain president rested. Over 100,000 people came during the 24-hour period that Lincoln remained. Here, the funeral coach drawn by a team of white horses prepares to move Lincoln.

22

ERIE STREET CEMETERY. The first municipal cemetery in Cleveland was located on Erie Street (now known as East 9th Street) and was called Erie Street Cemetery when it opened in 1826. Many of the city's original settlers were interred into the Erie Street Cemetery, such as Lorenzo Carter, who had died in 1814 and was moved to Erie Street Cemetery after 1840. The Gothic-style structure and hazy atmosphere ironically reflect the name of the cemetery.

ST. JOHN'S CATHEDRAL. The premier church for the Roman Catholic Diocese of Cleveland is St. John's Cathedral, located on Superior Avenue and East 9th Street. The cornerstone for the church was laid in 1849 during the tenure of the Reverend Amadeus Rappe, the first bishop of Cleveland's Catholic diocese. The church was formally dedicated in 1852. In this photograph, the church is seen without its massive steeple.

23

CENTENNIAL PUBLIC SQUARE. Numerous events, parades, and other festivities that continued for days marked the celebration of Cleveland's first 100 years as a city. On Superior Avenue at Public Square, an enormous arch was constructed to honor Cleveland's centennial. Built of wood and coated with white plaster, it stood 79 feet high, 106 feet wide, and 20 feet deep. Designed by W. Dominick Benes, it was built as an arch of triumph, suited to Cleveland's emergence as a major metropolis. To the right is the Soldiers and Sailors Monument, which replaced the Perry Monument as the city's leading landmark. The Soldiers and Sailors Monument was designed by Levi Scofield to honor the four branches to serve during the Civil War: Artillery, Navy, Infantry, and Cavalry. Atop the tall central column is Lady Liberty. The interior contains the names of all who died inscribed on the walls. The monument remains today. The tall structure at left is the Cuyahoga Building, a landmark that has since been razed.

Two

THE CUYAHOGA RIVER

THE MOUTH OF THE CUYAHOGA RIVER. The development of Cleveland into a commercial and industrial giant was influenced heavily by its location, bounded by the southern shore of Lake Erie and the northern end of the Cuyahoga River. As depicted in this mid-19th-century view of harbor activity, Cleveland would dominate the shipping industry of the Great Lakes region, which would lead in turn to Cleveland's rise as a major city.

SAILING ON THE RIVER. In this scene depicting river life in the early 19th century, riverboat traffic moves quietly along as new ships are assembled on the bank at the left. To the right are simple two-story buildings erected for commercial purposes. In time, more factories and warehouses would line the riverbanks, and railroad lines would parallel the growing industries.

CLEVELAND AS PORT-OF-CALL. By 1824, the Village of Cleveland had become a thriving port-of-call as well as the commercial center for all of Cuyahoga County. It was not an unusual sight for the Cuyahoga River or the lakefront to look like a sea of masts. With the opening of the Ohio and Erie Canal, debate centered on which was the more profitable trade outlet—Lake Erie or the Cuyahoga River.

CANAL ROAD. This is a 1922 photograph of Canal Road and West 3rd Street in the Flats as seen from Huron road near Vinegar Hill. The West 3rd Street Bridge, which crosses the Cuyahoga River, can be seen on the left. The railroad tracks are those of the Baltimore and Ohio Railroad. The warehouses that dotted the northern portion of Canal Road can be seen in the distance.

OUTFITTING THE SHIPS. Companies and businesses that provided goods and services to the shipping industry flourished along the Cuyahoga River. In this 1890 photograph, a cargo ship owned by the Ward's Detroit and Lake Superior Line is docked near the shops of J.W. Grover, Ship Chandlers/Sail Makers; E.R. Hull and Company; and John C. Hemmeter, Grocers.

27

FREIGHTER AT DOCK. Loading and unloading a ship's cargo, particularly if the ship was a freighter, always posed a difficult task requiring strenuous hand labor. In 1880, Alexander Brown invented a mechanical hoist to unload a ship's cargo, particularly that of iron ore. Seen here *c.* 1895 is a Great Lakes freighter on the right having its cargo unloaded at the dock near Buckley Boulevard.

ORE-CARRYING PIG BOATS. In this photograph *c.* 1880, cargo vessels called Pig Boats, which resembled giant inflatable rafts, were used in the transport of iron ore. At the height of the industrial revolution, Cleveland, which already dominated the iron and steel industry, merged this success with its dominance of the Great Lakes shipping industry to become a leader in iron ore trade.

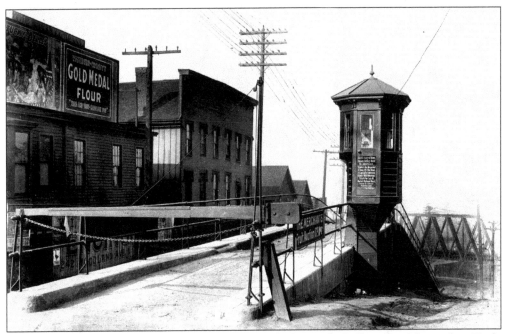

SMEAD'S ROLLING ROAD. The top level or east end of Smead's Rolling Road located on Eagle Avenue had a sign on the control tower which read: "Smead's Rolling Road. Visitors are requested to keep off the road. If especially interested confer with motorman. Tickets for sale at Market National Bank. Isaac D. Smead, Patentee and construction engineer."

THE ROLLING ROAD ENTRANCE. Often referred to as Cleveland's outdoor escalator, Smead's Rolling Road was located at the current location of the Eagle Avenue ramp, which leads down into the Flats. The Rolling Road was used by business and shipping companies to carry heavy loads and livestock from Canal Road in the Flats up to the Ontario Avenue street level.

NAVIGATING THE CROOKED RIVER. In this 1920 photograph, a little tug boat pulls an empty ore freighter back down the winding Cuyahoga River, which was known as the "crooked water" by Native Americans. The industrial character of the Flats is apparent as warehouses and factories stretch along the riverbank. The tall building in the center has written on the side, "Sherwin Williams Paints and Varnishes."

OVERVIEW OF THE FLATS. This 1910 photograph was taken from Scranton Heights, which was located on the west bank of the Cuyahoga River. On the left is the Columbus Road Bridge, which spans across the river and enters the Flats. At this time, Columbus Road extended as far north as Superior Avenue to where the Frank J. Lausche State Office Building would be built.

THE SUPERIOR AVENUE VIADUCT. In 1878, the Superior Avenue Viaduct opened for traffic as the first high-level bridge built across the Cuyahoga River. It was built to connect the east and west sides of Cleveland and to improve the commute. B.F. Morse engineered the viaduct with a center draw span, which as seen in this 1912 photograph turned to allow freighters and other tall river craft to pass underneath..

UNLOADING THE C.A. Black. In 1898, Clevelander George Hulett patented his electrically powered Hulett unloader. Designed like a clamshell bucket, the Hulett significantly reduced unloading time along with labor costs, which resulted in the building of larger, specially designed lake freighters. In this 1927 photograph, the freighter *Clarence A. Black* is being unloaded by a Hulett on the Cuyahoga River.

FUN IN THE FLATS. Life in the Flats was not limited to shipping and industry. Boaters often sailed their crafts leisurely down the Cuyahoga River, enjoying the beauty of the valley. Pleasure cruises were advertised, which included both daily excursions and overnight trips. As seen in this photograph from July 4, 1909, passengers walk up from the Flats after departing from a cruise ship belonging to the Detroit and Cleveland Navigation Company.

FIRE IN THE FLATS. On March 1, 1914, a fire broke out in the Fisher and Wilson Lumber Yard located in the Flats. It was a fire that raged on for 12 hours, destroying 20 acres of lumber yards and buildings and damaging the Central Viaduct. In this photograph, members of the Cleveland Fire Department pose after having successfully put out the fire.

Three

AN INDUSTRIAL GIANT

JOHN D. ROCKEFELLER (1839–1937). Oil magnate and America's first billionaire, J.D. Rockefeller came to Cleveland with his family in 1853 and worked as a commission merchant trading in farm staples like grain and pork. In this 1865 photograph, Rockefeller and partner Samuel Andrews, co-founder of the Standard Oil Company, opened their office in the Flats at Superior Avenue and Merwin Street near the Cuyahoga River, located to the right.

STANDARD OIL COMPANY OF OHIO, 1870. This is Refinery No. 1, built in 1863 in the early days of the oil industry. Equipment consisted mostly of wooden buildings and tubs into which crude oil was simply boiled to distill products such as kerosene, which was in general demand during this era. Processing capacity was about 10 barrels a day.

THE STANDARD OIL REFINERY, 1890. In 20 years, the wood buildings were replaced by an industrial complex that canvassed the Flats in the Cuyahoga Valley. The Flats, on the west bank of the Cuyahoga River, was an ideal location for commercial shipping and heavy industry including steel mills and oil refineries. Known as Standard Oil No. 1, this was the first refinery of John D. Rockefeller's industry.

A PASSION FOR GOLF. Oil may have made him a wealthy man, but golf gave John D. Rockefeller a passion for life. In this photograph, he engages in his favorite pastime at his Forest Hills Estate located in East Cleveland. It has been the family residence since 1878, and he kept it as a summer residence even after his move to New York City in 1888 for business reasons. Rockefeller would use Forest Hills as a summer residence until 1915.

ROCKEFELLER'S EUCLID AVENUE ADDRESS. When Rockefeller found success in the oil industry, he joined Cleveland's elite on "Millionaires' Row." Rockefeller purchased this Victorian home on Euclid Avenue and East 40th Street in 1868 for about $40,000. He and his wife, the former Laura Spelman, started their family of five children in this home and remained here until 1880. The house was razed in 1938.

THE WINSLOW HOME. Richard Winslow was an early settler who came to Cleveland c. 1820 and went into business as a grocery wholesaler, opening his store on Superior Avenue, then the commercial hub of the city. His home fronting the south side of Public Square on residential Euclid Avenue was an impressive two-story colonial built by Levi Johnson. When razed, this home would become part of the site of the May Company department store.

COMMERCIAL EUCLID AVENUE. Euclid Avenue began as a residential street until commerce forced its residents to move further east. In this 1890 photograph of the southeast corner of Public Square, the Perry Monument landmark stands left on the site of the Soldiers and Sailors Monument. Looking down Euclid Avenue, the street is lined on either side with commercial blocks for office and retail space.

THE MAY COMPANY. Euclid Avenue was the location of several successful department stores, such as the May Company, located here in 1899 in the original Ontario Avenue building at the southeast corner of Public Square. Cleveland's May Company was part of a retail chain based in Colorado and founded by David May. This building featured a clock tower and above the entranceway, a slogan that read, "Watch Us Grow." Indeed, by 1930, the May company of Cleveland would become Ohio's largest department store.

THE MAY COMPANY DELIVERS. The early May Company used a fleet of horse-drawn carriages for home deliveries. Here is delivery wagon No. 4 manned by a driver and his assistant as they pose in front of a modest home. The carriages featured an oval window and an attached lantern. The company logo and name are clearly marked on the side.

MILLIONAIRES' ROW. Wealthy residents built elaborate mansions along Euclid Avenue, otherwise known as Millionaires' Row. Nearly all of the homes are gone, razed as Euclid Avenue succumbed to commerce. These homes on the north side of Euclid Avenue, beginning at East 24th Street, belonged (left to right) to Samuel Bingham, Harry K. Devereux, Samuel Mather, Leonard C. Hanna, and Hickox-Brown. Only the Mather Mansion remains as part of Cleveland State University's campus.

THE FOUR-IN-HAND CLUB. Residents of Millionaires' Row were against traffic, other than horse-and-buggies, riding down their cobblestone road. Streetcars were diverted at Euclid Avenue and East 9th Street onto Prospect Avenue. In this May 1901 photograph, members of the Four-in-Hand Club take a leisurely stroll down Euclid Avenue at East 40th Street. Cleveland's elite continued to live here until 1910 when they began to move out and create more exclusive suburbs.

THE EELS MANSION. Dan Parmalee Eels (1825–1903) was a Cleveland banker and philanthropist who built this Victorian mansion at 3201 Euclid Avenue. Pictured here in 1880, the Eels Mansion incorporated many of the elements common to its neighbors. The mansion was removed some distance from the street to showcase the vast grounds and shrubbery and also to provide residents privacy. It had three floors, a central tower, and a flat roof.

THE FIRST METHODIST CHURCH. In 1874, the First Methodist Church was built at the corner of Euclid Avenue and East 9th (Erie) Street, which would become the future site of the landmark Cleveland Trust (Company) Building. Reflecting a Gothic style similar to neighboring mansions, the church remained at this location until a new church was constructed at Euclid Avenue and East 30th Street.

THE EVERETT MANSION. Sylvester T. Everett (1838–1922) was a Cleveland financier, railroad promoter, and city treasurer. This Romanesque-style mansion was built in 1883 on the northeast corner of Euclid Avenue and East 40th Street when Everett married Alice Louisa Wade, granddaughter of Jeptha Wade, an early Cleveland industrialist. The architect was Charles F. Schweinfurth (1856–1919), who first came to Cleveland on commission to design the elegant Everett mansion.

THE ANDREWS MANSION. The Victorian home of Samuel Andrews, an early business partner of John D. Rockefeller, was located on Euclid Avenue and East 30th Street. Reviews of this mansion have been mixed, with some admiring its grandeur and others appalled by what has been dubbed "Andrews Folly," an example of Victorian excess. Built in 1882, it had 33 rooms and required a staff of over 100 just to maintain. Andrews and his family lived in this home for only three short years.

THE WADE MANSION. The mansion of Jeptha H. Wade (1811–1890), Cleveland business and civic leader, was located on Euclid Avenue and East 40th Street (formerly known as Case Street). This stone mansion resembles the Tuscan villa style incorporated into the Rockefeller mansion on Euclid Avenue. Among its features are a flat roof and a front porch entrance flanked by two staircases.

THE ROOT AND McBRIDE COMPANY. Located on Lake Avenue at 1250 West 6th (Bank) Street northwest of Public Square in the Warehouse District, the six-story Root-McBride Building was erected in 1884 as a Victorian-style commercial complex. It housed the offices of Ralph R. Root and Leander McBride, successful wholesalers who began their trade in 1849 when they opened a small general dry-goods store.

THE WHITE COMPANY. Located in the industrial-rich Flats, the White Company was another Cleveland pioneer in automobile manufacturing. In 1900, Rollin White, invented the White Steamer automobile. Together with his brothers Windsor and Walter, they established the White Motor Car Company, manufacturers of automobiles and trucks. Their father, Thomas H. White, founded White Consolidated Industries, which created the famous white sewing machine.

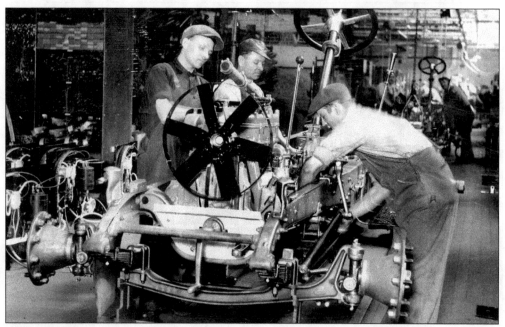

WHITE MOTOR COMPANY ASSEMBLY LINE. Cleveland became an industrial and manufacturing giant due, in large part, to the enormous contributions made by its factory workers, who often worked their entire adult lives for a single company. In this May 1928 photograph, assembly line factory workers (left to right) Mike Wazar, William Molchand, and William Frohlich are paying close attention to auto details.

ALEXANDER WINTON AND FRIENDS. Alexander Winton was an automotive pioneer who made Cleveland his home in 1884 when he left his native Scotland as a teenager. Three years after his arrival, he founded the Winton Motor Carriage Company, which continued producing automobiles until 1924. Seen here in 1896 is Winton (on the far left with his hand on the controls) taking a group of friends for a ride in his experimental two-cylinder car. Tom L. Johnson is seen on the right in the back seat.

STANDARD OIL WAGON WORKS. The Standard Oil Company was involved in a number of subsidiary businesses, outgrowths of its primary oil industries. In this photograph c. 1910, several workers pose in Standard's wagon works, which built wagons used to take Standard goods to buyers. The factory was located in the Flats.

THE GRASSELLI CHEMICAL COMPANY. In this photograph *c.* 1900, looking north towards Broadway Avenue are yard and city delivery vehicles belonging to the Grasselli Chemical Company. This company, named for Italian immigrant and skilled chemist Eugene R. Grasselli, provided chemicals to various industries. The brick building in the background on the right is a sulfuric acid chamber, and the long frame building is the ammonium chloride department.

THE AUSTIN POWDER COMPANY. One of the first of Cleveland's many manufacturing industries was the Austin Powder Company, pictured here on the Ohio and Erie Canal route near the five-mile lock. The Austin Company was founded in 1833 by brothers who lent their name to the business. They began by making blasting powder used in, among other things, building the canal. Later, the brothers turned their interests to using the powder for ammunition.

THE SHERWIN-WILLIAMS COMPANY. In 1866, Henry A. Sherwin (1842–1916) decided to invest in the newly emerging paint industry, and by 1870, Sherwin-Williams and Company had been organized. Sherwin entered into a partnership with Alanson T. Osborn and Edward P. Williams to establish their company. In this 1905 photograph, office workers put in another day at the company office on Canal Road. The name Sherwin-Williams would become synonymous with paint.

THE WARNER AND SWASEY COMPANY. In this 1914 photograph, employees of Warner and Swasey work in the tool room. Warner and Swasey manufactured precision instruments, telescopes, and tools, which were used in heavy machinery. The company opened shop in Cleveland in 1881 near East 55th Street and Carnegie Avenue. Demand for machine tools during the industrial age and World War I helped Warner and Swasey prosper. The company has since closed.

THE LENNOX BUILDING. As Euclid Avenue developed commercially, the intersection at East 9th Street and Euclid Avenue attracted many retail and banking businesses. In this photograph taken October 1919, the Lennox Building, erected 1889–1890, sits on the northeast corner of East 9th Street and Euclid Avenue. The architect was Charles Schweinfurth, who was quickly gaining a reputation as one of Cleveland's leading designers. Occupying ground-level storefronts are the Encyclopedia Britannica and Frances Willard Candies.

THE UNION TRUST BUILDING. The Lennox Building was razed in the early 1920s to make room for the Union Trust (Bank) Building on the left, which at 21 stories tall was considered one of the largest office buildings then in existence. Constructed during 1923–1924, it remained the Union Trust Building until banking ownership changed, and it became the Union Commerce (Bank) Building and decades later, the Huntington (Bank) Building.

THE CLEVELAND TRUST BUILDING. Cleveland is a city with many impressive landmarks, among the most notable is the Cleveland Trust Building, which is located on the southeast corner of East 9th Street and extends from Euclid Avenue around to Prospect Avenue. It rests on the site previously occupied by the First Methodist Church, which moved to East 40th Street and Euclid Avenue where a new church was dedicated in 1905. The Cleveland Trust Company was established in 1894 and soon became a leader among Midwest banks. The Cleveland Trust Building was designed to mirror the bank's estimable reputation. It was built c. 1907 based on the design of George Brown Post, architect of the New York Stock Exchange. The neoclassical style was typical for the period, which desired to lend grandeur and prestige to banking establishments. Among the more notable features of this building is a 61-foot Tiffany-glass rotunda perched 85 feet above the floor. The twin exteriors fronting Euclid Avenue and Prospect Avenue resemble an ancient temple with columns and pediments. The building is no longer in use, yet remains as a historic landmark.

FRIES, KLEIN, AND COMPANY. The oldest department store on Cleveland's west side was Fries, Klein, and Company, the forerunner of the Fries and Schuele Company. George Klein and Charles Fries were the proprietors of this dry-goods store located on West 25th (Pearl) Street. When the store opened for business in 1868, it sold patterned carpets, oil cloths, dry goods, and notions. The first wagon in their delivery fleet is on the right.

THE FRIES AND SCHUELE COMPANY. Located on West 25th Street across from the landmark West Side Market, the Fries and Schuele Company began *c.*1880 from a partnership between owner Charles Fries and employee Christian Schuele. In this 1905 photograph, the two-story frame building was replaced with a multi-story brick structure. Advertised as specials were quality shirts on sale for 59¢, reduced from 85¢, and dresses marked half price.

THE FISHER BROTHERS COMPANY. Food wholesalers from New York City, the Fisher Brothers Company opened several stores in Cleveland in 1907. With locations on the east and west sides of the city, this company became one of the largest grocers and later reorganized as Fisher Foods, Incorporated.

THE BAILEY COMPANY DEPARTMENT STORE. Bailey's Department Store in downtown Cleveland occupied a 10-story building on Ontario and Prospect Avenues next to the May Company. It was a major retailer that grew out of a partnership established in 1899 between businessman Louis Black and Charles Sunshine. In this 1910 photograph, several mothers and their young children in Victorian dress admire the display windows decorated for the season.

THE ARCADE. Cleveland is a city that boasts of many "firsts." In 1890, the first indoor shopping mall in the United States opened—the Arcade. The Arcade runs for 300 feet as it connects the busy commercial streets of Euclid Avenue and Superior Avenue. As seen here in 1895, the view looks toward Superior Avenue from Euclid Avenue past four floors of glass-fronted stores and offices. The Arcade had a light and airy feeling enhanced by an interior that rose 100 feet to a glass roof forming a pointed arch held aloft by wrought-iron supports. The balconies, railings, and lamp posts are made of wrought iron and solid brass. George H. Smith and John Eisenmann were the designers and engineers of the Arcade, which cost $876,000. The interior is 60-feet wide and 90-feet high (plus 10 feet for the arch). The main entrance is on Superior Avenue, which is very similar in design to the Euclid Avenue entrance. The Arcade remains one of Cleveland's outstanding landmarks.

50

Four

GETTING AROUND THE CITY

EUCLID AVENUE ARCADE ENTRANCE. The Arcade extends for 300 feet, connecting Euclid Avenue to Superior Avenue. Since Euclid Avenue is 12 feet higher than Superior, the Arcade was built with two ground floors connected by a staircase. In this 1928 photograph, the Arcade entrance is seen on the left as an elaborate rock arch beginning at ground level. Architects Smith and Eisenmann used the Romanesque-revival style for the Arcade's façade.

THE NEWBURGH "DUMMY" RAILROAD. Wealthier residents of the small community of Newburgh decided to build a railroad to provide easier access to downtown Cleveland. In this 1870 photograph, the steam-driven train belonging to the Newburgh and Kinsman Line is seen crossing the wooden trestle bridge erected over the creek and valley of Kingsbury Run, which extended from East 79th Street westward.

THE UNION PASSENGER DEPOT. In order to accommodate the increasing railroad traffic resulting in part from the Civil War, a new passenger depot was constructed during 1864–1866. The Union Passenger Depot was built at the foot of West 9th (Water) Street. It was an impressive feat of engineering—a massive stone station with an interior space 603 feet by 180 feet enclosed under a single roof and the largest enclosure in Cleveland.

ON THE WATERFRONT. This is the Cleveland lakefront, photographed in 1892, at the eastern approach to the Union Passenger Depot. It is a spectacular view of Cleveland's 19th century skyline. On the left, the Central Armory tower is visible as the entire structure gives the appearance of a medieval fortress. Small boats glide across Lake Erie, and on the horizon line, a passing train is barely visible.

PASSING THE TIME AWAY. What could be more relaxing than lying on a grassy knoll on a warm day listening to the hum of trains moving in and out of the Union Passenger Depot? This station would remain the pride of Cleveland until the 1920s when the Van Sweringen Brothers would build a massive Union Terminal Complex on Public Square.

CLEVELAND'S PREMIER ELECTRIC STREETCAR. As seen in this March 1890 photograph, passengers walk to board car No. 174 of the East Cleveland line at the intersection of Huron Road on the left and Prospect Avenue on the right, as they connect at East 9th (Erie) Street. The neighborhood is still residential, but in a few short years this triangle will be a busy commercial area.

STREETCARS TRANSFORM PUBLIC SQUARE. It was around 1884 when streetcars powered by electricity began to run in Cleveland. Horse-drawn streetcars were still in use, but they gradually gave way to electric-powered cars. In this photograph a two-car unit travels down Ontario Avenue ready to cross Superior Avenue on Public Square. In the background on the right, the steeple of the Old Stone Church is visible.

THE HORSE-DRAWN STREETCAR. Before the arrival of the electric-powered streetcars, a single horse or a team would pull the streetcar along a designated track line. Here, a winter car belonging to the Woodland Avenue and West Side Street Railway stops, perhaps on one of the streets serviced, Woodland Avenue, Pearl Street, or Lorain Streets.

A MANUAL TURNTABLE. Electric-powered streetcars used a "wye" for the turnaround at the end of a particular line. Horse-drawn streetcars changed direction with the help of a manned turntable. In this 1873 photograph, the man on the left holds a long stick, preparing to turn the approaching car on the left around once it has climbed onto the turntable.

BROADWAY AND NEWBURGH STREETCAR. Many streetcar lines ran through the streets of Cleveland. By 1890, four of these lines, East Cleveland, Brooklyn, the South Side, and Broadway and Newburgh, merged to form the Cleveland Electric Railway Company, which was also known as the Big Consolidated or Big Con. Here the conductor is at the switch iron waiting for some light cleaning to be done by the trolley boy who swept the car after each trip.

THE EAST CLEVELAND RAILROAD COMPANY. In this photograph *c.* 1890, a summer streetcar, featuring long benches and open sides, prepares to leave the Lake View Station carrying a total of seven passengers. This line would cover tracks along Euclid and Prospect Avenues. The East Cleveland Railway line was part of the merger leading to the organization of Big Consolidated.

OTTO BEHRENDT AT THE REINS. It was not often a streetcar conductor was identified by name. In the horse car days, Conductor Behrendt poses with his passengers and crew on West 25th Street at Clark Avenue. This is car No. 20 of the Brooklyn Street Railway, which merged with three other lines in 1893 to form the Cleveland Electric Railway Company.

THE MILES AVENUE STATION. When not in use, streetcars were berthed at stations similar to this one, c. 1900. This massive brick station was located at East 131 Street and Miles Avenue and featured a huge arch, seen on the right, with car No. 116 used by conductors on their break. Jutting out from the arch on the far left is car No. 66.

THE EUCLID AVENUE LINE. In this photograph, streetcar No. 288 travels east down the 7900 block of Euclid Avenue. This convertible streetcar is very sleek in style, with removable glass-paneled sides. Inside the car, some advertising is visible near the roof. The conductor remains standing outside, manually controlling the switch iron used in guiding the cars down the tracks.

THE TROLLEY KIDS. Streetcars and kids seemed to always go together as seen in this photograph from the early 1920s of the Brooklyn Station with a two-car West 25th Street train pulling into the station from Pearl Road. The sign posted below the window of car No. 664 is advertising a boxing match between Dempsey and Carpenter.

THE SCRANTON AVENUE RAILWAY LINE. The Scranton Avenue Railway Line was one of over a dozen streetcar lines operated by the Cleveland Electric Railway Company or Big Con. In this photograph *c.* 1910, the conductor poses beside streetcar No. 194, which will take passengers along Scranton, Clark, and Burton. Notice the prominent cowcatcher affixed to the front of the car.

THE BIG STEP. The streetcar was responsible for helping neighborhoods flourish, as businesses were built often parallel to the rail lines. On the left, several storefronts are visible, including a branch office of the *Plain Dealer* daily newspaper. In boarding car No. 1042, an attendant comes into the street to make sure the way is clear for the woman to safely get on board.

THE SUPERIOR AVENUE VIADUCT. Bridging the gap between Cleveland's east and west sides became possible with the opening of the Superior Avenue Viaduct, which crossed over the Cuyahoga River and the Flats. Before the completion of this bridge, traveling from one side of the city to the other could be arduous. When the bridge was swung shut, traffic flowed smoothly.

KAMM'S CORNER. In this photograph c. 1900, a Cleveland southwestern car is ready to make the turn onto Rocky River Drive, which formed Kamm's Corner at its intersection with Lorain Avenue. The area was named for Oswald Kamm, who in 1875, opened a small grocery store and served as the postmaster for Rockport Township.

THE SUBWAY STATION. At the intersection of West 25th Street and Lorain Avenue was the beginning of the entrance ramp leading to Cleveland's downtown subway station. As seen in this 1918 photograph, passengers board and depart a train bound for Lorain Avenue. The sign on the right advertises "Milkmens Day" at Luna Park.

THE BRIDGE APPROACH VIA DETROIT AVENUE. In this 1909 photograph, the view looks west toward Detroit Avenue, moving away from downtown Cleveland, at the intersection of West 25th Street. The approach to the Detroit-Superior High-Level Bridge will move east into downtown Cleveland with access to the subway station. The corner building on the left is the Forest City Savings and Trust Company.

THE DETROIT-SUPERIOR HIGH-LEVEL BRIDGE. As the Superior Avenue Viaduct proved unable to relieve traffic congestion, a high-level bridge was built over the Cuyahoga River and Valley. It was to be Cleveland's first high-level bridge and would ease traffic woes by connecting Detroit and Superior Avenues without bowing to river traffic. When the bridge opened in December 1917, the west side benefited as neighboring suburbs like Lakewood developed.

BUILDING A BRIDGE. In this construction photograph of the Detroit-Superior High-Level Bridge, huge cranes work to guide a section of the center steel arch into place. The bridge would cost over $5,000,000 to construct over a period of five years. A view of the industrialized Flats can be seen in the distance.

THE ARCH BEGINS TO TAKE SHAPE. When completed, the Detroit-Superior High-Level Bridge would rise 96 feet above the Cuyahoga River. The central arch would be 591-feet long, flanked at the outer ends by 12 concrete arches. Altogether, the length of the bridge alone would measure over 3,112 feet.

THE DETROIT-SUPERIOR BRIDGE WORK CREW. Dozens of crew members pose in front of their work-in-progress, the Detroit-Superior High-Level Bridge. When completed, some if not all of the crew will have spent a total of five years on the project.

BOARDING THE CLEVELAND-BEREA LINE. Public Square in 1910 was bustling with activity. It was a time when a trip to downtown Cleveland meant experiencing the best in retail, entertainment, and sightseeing. Men dressed in suits and ties and wearing straw hats would pedal around town as newsboys toted current events in a large cloth bag. It was also a time when Cleveland had six electric-car or interurban systems to take passengers on a high-speed ride to selected stops in the Greater Cleveland area. Interurban travel came to Cleveland in 1901 and became very popular with service continuing until 1938. Two Victorian-garbed women are seen boarding an interurban operated by the Cleveland, Southwestern, and Columbus Railway system bound for suburban Berea, southwest of Cleveland. The Southern Division of this interurban system would also take passengers from Cleveland to Brunswick, Strongsville, Seville, and Medina. Of interest in the background are three of Cleveland's most famous landmarks—the Soldiers and Sailors Monument on the left, the Cuyahoga Building directly behind the column, and the much taller Williamson Building.

WAITING AT THE "PAGODA" STATION. Passengers waiting to board a streetcar or interurban found the experience enhanced by waiting stations designed in the style of a Japanese pagoda. There were five such waiting stations constructed around Public Square, each one designed with Japanese-style sloping roofs and enclosed waiting room. These eye-pleasing landmarks remained on Public Square until around 1955, when streetcar travel had ended in the city.

RIDING AROUND THE SQUARE. In this photograph of downtown Cleveland *c.* 1910, the view is looking west towards Superior Avenue from the northeast quadrant as streetcar and pedestrian traffic, with an occasional horse and buggy, navigate around the four quadrants of Public Square. In the background on the left is one of the oldest hotels in Cleveland, Forest City House. It was demolished to make way for the Terminal Tower.

THE TRAFFIC TOWER. On the corner of East 9th (Erie) Street and Euclid Avenue stood the immense traffic tower, which turned out to be more of a hazard to pedestrians and motor vehicles than initially realized. In this 1924 photograph, the view is looking west up Euclid Avenue at East 9th Street towards Public Square. The traffic tower required an operator positioned inside the glass booth to manually change the traffic signals. The novelty of the tower attracted so much attention that pedestrians and drivers alike would ignore the signals as they passed by the tower. In 1931, the traffic tower was removed. Of particular interest is the car on the left, which is a Baker Electric. Walter C. Baker was a Cleveland automotive pioneer and founder of the Baker Motor Vehicle Company in 1898. He specialized in electric cars and developed left-handed steering. Also on the left is the Hippodrome Theater, one of the finest playhouses in Cleveland with state-of-the-art lighting and equipment and a seating capacity of over 3,500.

EAST 9TH STREET AND EUCLID AVENUE. In this photograph *c.* 1920, the view is at the intersection of East 9th Street and Euclid Avenue looking east. This was the busiest retail and commercial intersection after Public Square. On the left are the tall Doric columns of the Union Commerce Building; next door is the B.R. Baker Company; and just down the block is the Hotel Statler. Work cars can be seen repairing track.

THE SHAKER RAPID. Making the turn from Euclid Avenue onto East 9th Street below the traffic tower is a Shaker Heights Rapid Transit streetcar. This transit line began operating in 1920 and provided a route from downtown Cleveland to the suburb of Shaker Heights, a residential development of the Van Sweringen Brothers. At this time, Euclid Avenue was being abandoned by the wealthy in favor of more secluded neighboring suburbs.

EAST 9TH STREET PIER. In this photograph, passengers can be seen boarding and departing streetcar No. 308 at the East 9th Street Pier stop near the lakefront, c. 1920. In the background on the right is the new Cleveland City Hall. To the immediate left of City Hall, the tower belonging to the medieval-inspired Central Armory is visible.

PLOWING THROUGH A BLIZZARD. One of the worst snowstorms in the history of Cleveland occurred in November 1913. This blizzard nearly paralyzed the city, as businesses and residents worked for days clearing streets. In this photograph, an interurban bound from Cleveland to Berea navigates its way west down Superior Avenue.

HEADING FOR DOWNTOWN CLEVELAND. In this 1909 photograph, streetcar No. 599 travels north down residential West 73rd Street towards Clark Avenue, which will lead to downtown Cleveland and Public Square. The Clark Line was one of many streetcar lines that merged to create the Cleveland Electric Railway Company or Big Con. Clark Avenue was one of the west side's oldest streets, which became an avenue *c.* 1870.

STREETCAR FAIR ON PUBLIC SQUARE. Cleveland played host to an impressive streetcar fair in 1928 that was located next to the Public Auditorium on Lakeside and St. Clair Avenues across from City Hall, which is barely visible in the background on the left. Row after row of streetcars (both horse-powered and electric), interurbans, and even locomotives were on display.

3¢ FARE LINE. Tom L. Johnson, perhaps Cleveland's most progressive mayor, started a 3¢ line in 1906 on Fulton Avenue on the city's west side to compete against a rival 5¢ line operated by the Cleveland Electric Railway Company. At the height of the "Streetcar War," Johnson's Forest City Railway line laid a temporary track on Superior Avenue, west of Public Square. In 1907, Johnson had won the battle.

THE STREETCAR STRIKE OF 1899. In June 1899, workers of the Big Consolidated streetcar line, demanding higher wages and better working conditions, decided to strike against the Cleveland Electric Railway Company, which owned and operated Big Con. The strike lasted several months, involving strikebreakers and riots. In the end, the workers lost, and many were allowed to return to their jobs. Many streetcars, like the one seen here, were damaged.

Five

MUNICIPAL AFFAIRS

JOHNSON'S "RED DEVIL." Cleveland mayor and streetcar magnate Tom L. Johnson is often regarded as the best mayor in Cleveland history. Here, he rides in his own 1903 Red Devil, a creation of the Winton Motor Company. At the wheel is Loftin Johnson, the mayor's son, and in the rear is Johnson's driver. Mayor Johnson led Cleveland in its most progressive era in politics and civic development.

CITY HALL CONSTRUCTION. Ever since Cleveland appeared on the map, buildings have been constructed incorporating the very latest in architectural design and construction innovation. Yet, Cleveland's city government continued to operate from temporary housing, dutifully paying rent, until construction of a new City Hall was approved. Here a crew of workers pose for this photograph on September 18, 1914.

CLEVELAND CITY COUNCIL, 1925. Cleveland was a progressive city and included among its council members the first elected African-American councilman, Thomas W. Fleming (second row, fourth from right) and the first elected women, Miss Marie Remington Wing (left) and Mrs. Helen H. Green (right). At the time, Cleveland was under the City Manager form of government wherein council also selected a mayor to preside over the meetings.

CITY COUNCIL CHAMBER. The interior of Cleveland's city council chamber is a multi-level room richly paneled in solid oak with observation galleries at each end. In this 1922 photograph, the chamber is filled with council members and members of the general public. Councilman Thomas Fleming is seated at the far left, first row.

THE CITY MANAGER PLAN. In 1924, the city manager form of government went into effect in Cleveland—the largest city in the nation to adopt this system. Voters approved the plan in 1921, which replaced city wards with districts and gave council the task of choosing both the city manager and the mayor. This system of government remained in place until 1931. Pictured here in 1929 is William R. Hopkins (seated left), Cleveland's first city manager.

THE TRAFFIC LIGHT. When Garrett A. Morgan arrived in Cleveland in 1895, he worked for small businesses while nurturing his ingenuity to invent. In 1923, Morgan received a patent for a hand-operated traffic signal, which used three lights for stop, go, and warning. This photograph shows the intersection of Euclid Avenue and East 105th Street where the first traffic signals were installed, near the point where two streetcars intersect.

GARRETT A. MORGAN AND THE GAS MASK. Garrett Morgan (1877–1963) was an African-American inventor most notable for inventing a breathing apparatus, or gas mask, which he used to rescue workers trapped in Cleveland's waterworks tunnel disaster. Born in Kentucky, Morgan moved to Cincinnati while still a teenager. He received only a few years of public schooling before setting off on his own. His drive and creativity led Morgan to invent numerous devices. When an explosion under Lake Erie in July 1916 killed nearly two dozen workers, Morgan entered the tunnel under the lake wearing the gas mask he models in the photograph. His daring and inventiveness saved several workers. Garrett Morgan had his gas mask patented in 1914.

CHARLES FRANCIS BRUSH (1849–1929). On April 29, 1879, Cleveland's Public Square became the site of the world's first public, electric street lighting designed by Brush, inventor of the arc light. By 1882, his light was adopted by cities worldwide. In this photograph, Brush is in his Euclid Avenue home laboratory inspecting his apparatus for measuring the rate at which objects fall. His goal was to upset Einstein's famous theory.

CLEVELAND ELECTRIC ILLUMINATING COMPANY (CEIC). Charles Brush, inventor and pioneer in electric lighting, is often cited as one of the founders of CEIC. Brush helped found the Brush Electric Light and Power Company in 1880, following the success of his arc light. After a series of mergers and acquisitions involving Brush Electric, CEIC was incorporated in 1892. Here is the company located in the Flats.

THE CLEVELAND POLICE. The Metropolitan Police Act of 1866 led to the organization of a police board of commissioners and an increase in the number of police officers in the department. At the time, there were approximately 60 police officers spread out over four precincts. Police officers such as the ones pictured here would walk their beat in an effort to quiet any civil disobedience.

THE CENTRAL STATION, FIRST PRECINCT. The First Precinct of the Central Police Station was located on Champlain Street, which ran southwest of Public Square. This station, as well as the entire block, gave way to the construction demands of the Cleveland Union Terminal Tower Complex, built by the Van Sweringen Brothers in the late 1920s.

THE SEVENTH PRECINCT STATION. Early police stations resembled little more than modest frame single- or two-story buildings such as the one shown here, located on Wake Street near Harvard Street in downtown Cleveland.

CLEVELAND MOUNTED POLICE. The Mounted Unit of the Cleveland Police Department was one of the oldest in the nation with 100 years of service until budget woes discontinued the unit in 2003. Mounted police had always patrolled the downtown area as well as lent their presence during special public events drawing large crowds. Pictured here are Traffic Commissioner E.J. Donahue and Patrolman James Matowitz on horseback.

THE CLEVELAND FIRE DEPARTMENT. Cleveland's Fire Department was organized in May 1836 to include a chief engineer, two assistant engineers, two fire wardens, and a fire engine, which was little more than a hook-and-ladder apparatus. The Cleveland Fire Department is seen here manning the hoses as they respond to a downtown fire in February 1902. Cleveland firemen were accustomed to using horse and buggy to carry men and equipment to fire emergencies.

THE COLLINWOOD FIRE. On March 4, 1908, fire erupted shortly after 9 a.m. at Lakeview Elementary School on East 152nd Street in Collinwood. The fire completely gutted the school building and killed 174 people, 172 of whom were children. It was determined the fire began in the basement under the front stairway. Panic caused the children to become trapped in the doorway. This school would replace the fire-ravaged building.

MEMORIAL SCHOOL. Pictured here is Memorial School teacher Mrs. Lucille Miller with her class of 36 children, housed for the winter in an ill-equipped cottage on the school grounds. There were five such cottages at Memorial School erected as temporary classrooms after the tragedy of the Collinwood school fire.

CLEVELAND FIRE TRUCK. Cleveland firefighters in 1912 were given their first automotive fire truck at the Ashbury Station on East 122nd Street. When fire protection was first introduced to Cleveland, volunteers were enthusiastic when a fire engine operated by hand was introduced to the department in 1829. In May 1836, the fire department was formally organized.

CENTRAL HIGH SCHOOL. The first Central High School was a modest frame structure erected in 1846. The school pictured above was built in 1878 for $74,000 and designed by Levi T. Scofield, architect of the Soldiers and Sailors Monument. It is a three-story Victorian-Gothic building with an impressive clock tower.

CENTRAL HIGH SCHOOL CLASS. Central High School's 1895 Girls' Literary Club is dressed in proper Victorian attire. Central High was Cleveland's first public high school. A bronze plaque near the school's entrance was dedicated by the alumni of the class of 1921, reads in part, "The First Free High School West of the Alleghenies." It was a tuition-free school.

TREMONT SCHOOL BAND. In this photograph *c.* 1912 are junior members of the Tremont School orchestra. Public education in Cleveland attempted to incorporate music study and appreciation into the curriculum in order to produce a better-educated and well-rounded student. The students here pose proudly as they await an opportunity to show their musical skills.

TREMONT SCHOOL. Tremont public school was located in the Tremont neighborhood of Cleveland on the west side. Tremont's location near the Cuyahoga River made it suitable for industry, and the neighborhood was primarily a working-class community heavily populated by immigrants representing German, Irish, and Polish ethnic groups. Tremont School was an imposing three-story brick structure, simple in design, reflecting the hard-working qualities of the residents.

THE CENTRAL MARKET. The first market to open in the city of Cleveland was Central Market in 1867. It was located on Ontario Avenue across from Eagle Avenue, which led down to the Flats. When Central Market opened, stalls were available to accommodate over 200 vendors. By 1890, the city's increasing population rendered the market obsolete, and plans were underway for a new market house. Fire destroyed the building in 1949.

THE SHERIFF STREET MARKET. Located in downtown Cleveland on East 4th Street between Huron and Bolivar Avenues, Sheriff Street Market opened in 1890 as the city's largest market. It was owned and operated by the Sheriff Street Market and Storage Company. Designed by Lehman and Schmitt, the market featured a huge center aisle, twin six-story towers, and room for outdoor stalls. The market was sold in 1929.

THE WEST SIDE MARKET. Located on West 25th Street and Lorain Avenue, this market was the world's largest indoor market when it opened in 1912. Owned by the city of Cleveland, the market was designed to host 100 vendors indoors and an additional 85 vendors outside.

SHOPPING AT THE WEST SIDE MARKET. In this 1915 photograph, a woman pauses by one of the many vendors located inside the main concourse of the market. At the market, a wide variety of foods representing the diversity of ethnic cultures of Cleveland's west side could be found and prepared to the customer's request. At one time, live chickens were slaughtered on the spot. Health codes have since discontinued the practice.

JANE EDNA HUNTER (1882–1971). Jane Edna Hunter was an African-American social worker who became the founder and director of the Phyllis Wheatley Association in 1911. Named for the African-American poet, the Wheatley Association provided social services, recreation, and additional assistance for young women and girls residing in the area of East 44th Street and Cedar Avenue. Jane Edna Hunter came to Cleveland in 1905 where she worked as a nurse. She later received a law degree in Cleveland and used her skills to work towards improving opportunities for women.

ALTA HOUSE. Located on East 125th Street and Mayfield Road in an area known as Little Italy, Alta House opened in 1901 as a social settlement house for Italian immigrants. The idea for Alta House, named for patron John D. Rockefeller's daughter, was introduced by marble importer Joseph Carabelli. Alta House would help Carabelli workers make the transition into American life. Charles Hopkinson designed the large, red brick structure.

LEARNING THE LANGUAGE. Immigrants who settled in America worked hard to become assimilated in their adopted culture. The surest way to become an American was to properly learn the language. Classes were often held at social settlement houses, in local schools, or as seen in this photograph c. 1895, at the YWCA, which offered educational programs to help young women find employment. Here a group of women are learning the basics of table etiquette. They each have been given a copy of the chart displayed on the wall, which lists all the china and utensils needed to set a proper table. As stated on the chart, this is the fifth lesson where the women are taught English using such phrases as, "the dining room table is square," or "the table is made of wood." The lesson is highlighted by the instructor seated at a wooden table set for four to demonstrate the practicality of the lesson. When the lesson program is completed, the young women will possess the skills to work in a private home or a restaurant.

IMMIGRATION LABOR OFFICE. Cleveland would not have developed into the city it had without the talent and support of its many ethnic groups. In this c. 1900 photograph of Cleveland's Immigration Labor Office, the room is packed with men, young and old, skilled and unskilled workers, seeking employment. Because Cleveland was an industrial and manufacturing giant, it would not be very difficult to place many of these workers in factory jobs.

HIRAM HOUSE. The first social settlement house built in Cleveland was Hiram House, which was located on Orange Avenue. George A. Bellamy and students from Hiram College who desired to help neighborhood immigrants assimilate organized Hiram House in 1896. Unlike its counterpart Alta House, Hiram House was razed.

ST. STANISLAUS CATHOLIC CHURCH. Located on East 65th Street and Forman Avenue near the Cleveland Rolling Mills, St. Stanislaus Church was the first parish organized by the city's Roman Catholic Polish residents. St. Stanislaus parish came together in 1873, but the church itself would not be completed until 1881. Like many neighborhood churches, St. Stanislaus was built by the parishioners near the primary place of employment and residence. It was a church built to celebrate the rich heritage of the large Polish community. The first pastor was Father Anton F. Kolaszewski. In this 1909 photograph, the church had sustained storm damage.

CHERRY STREET. Cleveland's Cherry Street provides a look at the kind of immigrant housing typically found in the city. Streets were often plotted by developers to conform to the needs of neighboring factories and businesses, which required that workers live nearby. As seen here, the homes were typically simple wooden-frame buildings, no more than two or two-and-a-half stories tall, with a gabled end facing the street, and a front porch.

St. Colman's Catholic Church. St. Colman's Church is located at the corner of West 65th Street and Lorain Avenue, a predominantly Irish neighborhood. As seen in 1928, St. Colman's is a massive stone structure featuring twin towers. The architect was William Ginther. The original St. Colman's was a wooden frame building topped by a small cross.

Interior of St. Colman's Church. Many skilled artisans lent their talent and energy to building the beautiful interior of St. Colman's. In this 1928 photograph, the first floor of the church has an altar flanked by beautifully carved marble statues. The detailed marble and terrazzo flooring was laid by Italian artist Vincent (Vincenzo) Belfi, president and owner of the Union Marble and Mosaic Company.

CARNEGIE-WEST BRANCH LIBRARY. The Carnegie-West Library is located on Fulton Road at Lorain Avenue. It was the first branch library opened as part of the Cleveland Public Library System. Carnegie-West first opened in 1892 in rented quarters on West 25th Street. This building opened in 1910 with the financial assistance of Andrew Carnegie, who used his wealth to help found community libraries. The architect was New Yorker Edward L. Tilton, who specialized in designing libraries.

BROADWAY BRANCH LIBRARY. The Cleveland Public Library System includes the main library located on Superior Avenue, once ranked as the third largest library in the nation and still one of the finest nationwide, and nearly 30 branch libraries situated throughout Cleveland's neighborhoods. The Broadway Branch is located on Broadway Avenue and features an entranceway flanked by two massive stone columns and bronze doors.

ST. VINCENT'S ORPHANAGE. Located on the west side at Fulton Road and Monroe Avenue, St. Vincent's Orphanage, also called St. Vincent's Orphan Asylum, was first opened in 1852 by the Catholic Charities of Cleveland. The brick building seen here was completed in 1865 to house 100 orphaned boys and boys from poor families, aged four to fourteen. St. Vincent's Orphanage closed in the early 1920s.

SCHOOL PLAYGROUND CHILDREN. Children attending Cleveland's many public schools benefited from the efforts of various school and other educational associations that provided playground equipment for recreation. In this 1916 photograph, children on Woodland Avenue wait patiently for a chance on the swing, part of the equipment provided by the Educational Alliance.

CLEVELAND CITY HOSPITAL. Cleveland's City Hospital was established in 1866 on Lake Avenue following the end of the Civil War when returning veterans needed a hospital for rest and recovery. In 1875, the hospital received a new name, Lakeside Hospital. It grew out of a Protestant recovery effort to provide not only hospital care, but also a shelter for those left homeless by the war.

MOUNT SINAI HOSPITAL. Mount Sinai Hospital was dedicated in September 1916 at 1800 East 105th Street. The organization of Mount Sinai Hospital began with the Young Ladies Hebrew Association, a charitable organization begun in 1892 by Herman Sampliner. In 1900, the organization assumed the name Jewish Women's Hospital Society. The first president of Mount Sinai Hospital was Paul L. Feiss. The hospital has since closed.

THE YMCA/Y-TECH. In this 1928 photograph, the Johnson Building is used to house Y-Tech, the Young Men's Christian Association School of Technology. The YMCA of Cleveland was originally founded in 1854 on West 3rd Street and Superior Avenue. In 1867 with the help of Sereno Peck Fenn, a founder of Sherwin-Williams, the organization grew and by 1921 occupied new quarters at East 22nd Street and Prospect Avenue.

YWCA GIRLS. Building a campfire on a sandy beach is fun for these members of the Young Women's Christian Association. Originally founded in 1868 as the Women's Christian Association of Cleveland, its purpose was to promote the moral health and physical welfare of young women, particularly those who were single urban dwellers. In 1893, the organization became known as the YWCA and was located on West 3rd Street and Superior Avenue.

Six

ENTERTAINING CLEVELAND

PHIL SELZNICK AND RADIO WHK. WHK represents the call letters of not only Cleveland's, but also Ohio's first radio station, which debuted in 1922 as station 8 ACS from a Payne Avenue amateur home theater belonging to Warren Cox. Music filled the airwaves and introduced listeners to talented entertainment provided by Phil Selznick, seen here in 1929 in the station's new studio on the southeast corner of Ontario and St. Clair Avenues.

LUNA PARK. This 35-acre amusement park opened in 1905 on a site bordered by East 110th Street, Woodhill Road, and Woodland Avenue. Fred Ingersoll, a contractor from Pittsburgh who specialized in building amusement park rides, built Luna Park. Pictured here are Luna Park's vaudeville performers enjoying a ride on the Great Aerial Swing. The Swing featured a decoratively fringed top, which typified Ingersoll's eclectic design scheme for Luna Park.

LUNA PARK'S ROLLER COASTER. What could be more thrilling than taking a roller coaster ride, especially on a wooden track? These enthusiastic riders of 1910 have just descended a large hill and appear ready to tackle another. The roller coaster featured 10 cars seating two across and a single bar for support. Of particular interest is the daring rider in the fifth car who is standing.

LUNA PARK'S SHOOT THE CHUTE. Luna Park patrons enjoy the thrill of a roller coaster combined with a boat ride on the park's Shoot the Chute amusement in 1906. The theater building is to the left of the ride, standing as a small replica of India's Taj Mahal. In front of the theater is the Infant Incubator exhibit which treated premature babies for free using techniques not practiced in hospitals.

EUCLID BEACH PARK. Euclid Beach was a popular amusement park located less than 10 miles from downtown Cleveland in the vicinity of East 156th Street. As it bordered Lake Erie's southern shore, patrons were offered the opportunity to visit the beach and enjoy the many rides and attractions. In this photograph c. 1912, streetcars from the St. Clair Avenue line move along the track running parallel to the pony track.

LEAGUE PARK. The first game at League Park, located at East 66th Street and Lexington Avenue, was played in May 1891. In this photograph *c.* 1922, baseball fans crowd around entranceways A and B, eager to pay 75¢ to watch their favorite teams. Imagine going to a game wearing a suit and tie as these fans are doing. Only one police officer was needed to control this group.

EDGEWATER PARK. Located on Cleveland's west side, along the southern shore of Lake Erie, Edgewater Park featured a dance pavilion as seen here in this 1920 photograph. Cleveland purchased the park in 1894 from industrialist Jacob B. Perkins. The park also provided a bath house, baseball diamond, as well as picnic and playground areas.

CLEVELAND AIR RACES. The first women's air derby was held in 1929 in Cleveland. Louise Thaden won the first women's air derby when she flew her Travelair biplane from Santa Monica, California, to the Cleveland National Air Races in 20 hours, 2 minutes, and 2 seconds.

ICE BOATING ON LAKE ERIE. Winter fun often included a ride across Lake Erie in a small sailing craft, as these two hearty boating enthusiasts demonstrated in 1908. They are gliding across the frozen lake on a craft resembling a catamaran and guided by two white sails. Cleveland's lakefront was enhanced by the presence of the lighthouse seen in the background to the right.

THE CLEVELAND MUSEUM OF ART. Located at 11150 East Boulevard in University Circle, the Cleveland Museum of Art remains one of the finest institutions of its kind in the world. The museum opened in June 1916 on four acres of property donated by industrialist Jeptha H. Wade. Architects Hubbell and Benes designed the $1.25 million museum, which has cleared land for a lagoon and promenade.

WADE PARK. University Circle, the cultural center of Cleveland, rests on land donated to the city in 1882 by prominent Clevelander Jeptha H. Wade. Bearing his name, Wade Park included 63 acres of the finest property for recreational activities. In this photograph, a lake is an added attraction to the area. In the background on the right is Adelbert College, an undergraduate school for men on the campus of Western Reserve University.

ADELLA PRENTISS HUGHES AND FRIENDS. The Cleveland Orchestra has retained its reputation as one of the finest in the world since it was organized in 1918 by wealthy socialite Adella Prentiss Hughes. In this 1924 photograph, Hughes, then business manager of the orchestra, stands next to Nikolai Sokoloff, the musical director, in the Masonic Hall where the orchestra will record *Finlandia* by Sibelius and the *Blue Danube Waltz* by Strauss.

THE WHK ORCHESTRA. Radio WHK's musical selections and accompaniments were provided by this small chamber group consisting of a violinist, cellist, pianist, and two organists, one of whom was Mrs. Max Schmidt. The group was photographed in May 1924 in a small room with draped ceiling and walls to soundproof the area from unwanted noise.

THE ALVIN THEATER. Located on Ontario Street across the street from the Central Market, Cleveland's first nickelodeon premiered in 1913. For 5¢, patrons could see the feature *Broncho Billy's Grit* accompanied by a player piano or organ. The Alvin Theater was one of many downtown theaters offering Clevelanders the novelty of a moving picture show.

INSIDE THE ALLEN THEATRE. The Allen Theater was one of five theaters that made up Cleveland's Playhouse Square, an entertainment district located on Euclid Avenue and East 14th Street. The Allen Theater opened c. 1921 as a movie house featuring live emcees. Seen here at center stage is a wedding party with musical accompaniment. Notice the sumptuous satin curtains highlighting the stage.

THE PLAYHOUSE SQUARE DISTRICT. By the early 1920s, Cleveland had gained a reputation as a major metropolitan area, as the "sixth city," and desired a cultural climate that would attract even more visitors to the area. Euclid Avenue was the only choice to host a series of theaters, fine restaurants, and retail stores similar to those found in New York City or Chicago. The five theaters that formed the heart of this district, all of which were opened between 1920–1922, were the Allen Theater, the Ohio Theater, the State Theater, the Palace Theater, and two Loews' Theaters. The Allen Theater opened in the eight-story Bulkley Building at 1501 Euclid Avenue, which leased commercial and office space. The feature playing opening week at the Allen, as seen in the photograph, was *The Greatest Love*. Next door to the Allen Theater stood the Ohio Theater and Loews State Theater.

CELEBRATING ARBOR DAY. Arbor Day celebrations, as the one seen here in 1912, were held annually to raise awareness about keeping the city beautiful and to offer an opportunity to have outdoor fun. Here, the children of Newton D. Baker, Cleveland mayor from 1912–1916 and later secretary of war under President Woodrow Wilson, are ready to do their part to keep Cleveland growing.

THE ZOO AT BROOKSIDE PARK. On the west side of Cleveland, at the intersection of Fulton Road and Denison Avenue, one of the city's first parks was opened in 1894. Brookside Park provided the area with picnic facilities, a baseball field, and a petting zoo, which as seen in this 1909 photograph was particularly popular with children.

GORDON PARK BEACH. What could be more relaxing than a day at the beach? Here a crowd of bathers and onlookers enjoy summer fun at Gordon Park. This 122-acre park situated east of Cleveland was named for prominent Cleveland businessman William J. Gordon (1818–1892), one of the founders of the Cleveland Iron Mining Company. Gordon purchased the land in 1865 and gave the park to the city upon his death.

THE JOHN PHILIP SOUSA BAND. Everyone loves a parade! Cleveland was honored to have perhaps the most famous band in history march down its streets as thousands lined up to see and hear the Sousa band on parade. Composer Sousa is best remembered for his rousing tune, *The Stars and Stripes Forever.* The band marched together with Clevelanders preparing to leave during World War I.

The Lyric Theater. The Lyric Theater was located on the northeast corner of East 9th Street and Bolivar Avenue. The building itself had been a church converted for theater use. Vaudeville productions were routinely featured with matinees shows playing for 10¢ admission, and evening shows for 20¢. The playbills advertise Weston and Raymond Company in *A Comedy of Errors* and Wyman and Ross in *Two Germans, That's All*.

Inside the Lyric Theater. Like many of the theaters and playhouses of Cleveland, ample seating was required to satisfy the growing number of patrons eager to take in the newest in entertainment. The interior of the Lyric Theater featured seating on the main floor, in the side gallery, and in the upper balcony. The upper floor walls and the ceiling were elaborately decorated with intricate designs.

Seven

BUILDING A
BETTER FUTURE

CLEVELAND ENTERS THE 20TH CENTURY. As Cleveland entered the next millennium, the population soared to over 560,000, earning it the title, the "Sixth City." By 1929, the population would approach nearly 1,000,000. Cleveland was a major American metropolis experiencing a downtown building boom, which added such towering structures as the Williamson Building, seen here on the left directly behind the Soldiers and Sailors Monument.

THE CLEVELAND PRESS NEWSBOYS. These enterprising young fellows are enthusiastic about getting the news out to Cleveland. The *Cleveland Press* began publication in 1878 as the *Penny Press*, which appealed to working-class subscribers. Edward W. Scripps founded the paper, which in 1889 was renamed the *Cleveland Press*. By 1903, the *Cleveland Press* had become the city's major paper.

THE SPANISH-AMERICAN WAR. In this 1898 photograph, Clevelanders welcome troops returning from the Spanish-American War. The public was so interested in the conflict that subscriptions for the *Cleveland Press* surpassed 100,000 and continued to climb. As President William McKinley was from Ohio, Clevelanders enthusiastically supported the conflict, sending over 1,000 troops primarily from the 5th Regiment of the Ohio National Guard to war.

THE GRAND ARMY OF THE REPUBLIC. This organization of Civil War veterans assembled on Public Square during the first week of September 1901 for a gala celebration. September 7th, the day after Clevelander Leon Czolgosz shot President McKinley, black crepe was hung and the festivities muted. In the background on the right stand three landmarks: the Cuyahoga building, the Williamson, and the Soldiers and Sailors Monument.

A PARADE OF NURSES. Perhaps the grandest celebration to grace Public Square was the centennial. In this 1896 photograph, nurses wearing long-sleeved, floor-length white ruffled dresses with white caps adorning upswept hair march side-by-side past the Cuyahoga Building on Superior Avenue and Public Square. The nursing community was well represented in Cleveland and proud of the fact that modern nursing in Ohio began here.

THE CENTRAL ARMORY. Located on Lakeside Avenue at East 6th Street, the Central Armory with its characteristic bell tower was built in 1893 by Cuyahoga County primarily to house members of the National Guard. When not used as military quarters, the Central Armory would host large public events, since it was such a large closed hall. Resembling a medieval fortress, the armory was designed by Lehman and Schmitt.

FROM THE HALLS OF THE CENTRAL ARMORY. Clevelanders were always ready to crowd downtown streets and give a grand farewell to their soldiers, as they are doing here in 1917. Members of the 5th Regiment of the Ohio National Guard are parading from the Central Armory on their way to the Union Depot, where this unit will become part of the 145th Infantry during the First World War.

RIDING INTO WAR. Thousands of Clevelanders, many of them family and friends, descend upon the Union Depot platform to say farewell to members of Company F as they head off to war aboard the Pennsylvania rail lines. An immediate impact of the war upon the city was an end to European immigration. Ironically, many of the Clevelanders who went to fight were of European descent.

THE CHAMBER OF COMMERCE. The Chamber of Commerce was established in 1893 in order to attract and promote business and civic interests in Cleveland. The efforts put forth by this organization helped establish Cleveland as a major city and the sixth largest as it entered the 20th century. This classical-style building stood next to the Society for Savings Bank on the northeast corner of Public Square.

THE HURON ROAD TRIANGLE. In this 1912 photograph, the triangle where Euclid Avenue, Huron Road, and East 14th Street intersect is seen. Following the end of World War I, developer Joseph Laronge looked to transform this area into a theater district. Together with Marcus Loew of Loew's Theaters in New York, vaudeville, movies, and live theater teamed with upscale shops to create a showplace that would attract visitors downtown.

THE PROSPECT AVENUE TRIANGLE. Cleveland's business district continued moving eastward down Euclid Avenue and away from Public Square. As a result, the intersection of Euclid Avenue and East 9th Street and Prospect Avenue began to prosper. When, in 1900, philanthropist Benjamin Rose built the 10-story Rose Building at 2060 East 9th Street, it was the largest office in Ohio. This 1921 photograph shows how the triangle has developed since then.

THE STRAND PICTURE THEATER. In this photograph c. 1920, the Erie Building is seen on the southeast corner East 9th Street and Prospect Avenue. It was home to the Strand Motion Picture Theater, one of Cleveland's earliest movie houses. On the left, the Hotel Winton, named for automotive pioneer Alexander Winton, can be seen. On the right is a portion of the building that would become the New York Spaghetti House.

DEVELOPING PROSPECT AVENUE. At the intersection of East 9th Street and Prospect Avenue, business and retail flourished after World War I. In this 1920 photograph, a policeman guides pedestrians and motor vehicles through the busy corner. Right of center is the Osborn Building, which houses the Lake Shore Bank. On the right is the Strand Picture Theatre, and in the background, new construction is seen with the Hotel Huron.

111

THE GROUP MALL PLAN. The idea of developing the mall area near the lakefront into a collection of similarly designed government buildings was born during the administration of Mayor Tom L. Johnson. There are many who regard this plan of 1903 to be among Johnson's greatest achievements. When completed in the 1920s, the Cuyahoga County Courthouse on the left, the Public Auditorium in the center, City Hall on the left in the background, as well as the Federal Building, the main branch of the Cleveland Public Library, and the Board of Education administration building would be built around the rectangular-shaped mall. The construction of City Hall began in 1912 and was formally dedicated in 1916. Located on Lakeside Avenue at East 6th Street, it was the first time Cleveland's city government had a new facility and not rented quarters. It was designed by J. Milton Dyer in a classical style and is the near twin of the courthouse. The Public Auditorium (or Hall) on the east side of the mall was completed in 1922 and was one of the largest auditoriums built at the time.

THE CUYAHOGA COUNTY COURTHOUSE. Opened to the public in 1912, the courthouse was designed by Lehmann and Schmitt, a Cleveland architectural firm. The building's classical style features a row of Doric columns on the upper façade, above which are six sculptures representing historical lawmakers. Placed as sentries on either side of the front steps are the seated bronze figures of Alexander Hamilton and Thomas Jefferson.

THE FEDERAL BUILDING. Located on the northeast corner of Superior Avenue, the Federal Building, which houses the U.S. Post Office, the U.S. Custom House, and federal court house, was completed in 1911. Architect Arnold Brunner was an original member of the Group Plan Commission responsible for developing the mall. The Federal Building is of classical design, and its façade is flanked on either corner by statues representing commerce and industry.

LAKEFRONT VIEW OF THE MALL. In this 1929 aerial photograph, the Group Mall Plan is seen from Lake Erie. On the left of Lakeside Avenue in the foreground is City Hall and on the right in the foreground is the Cuyahoga County Courthouse. At 500-feet wide, the mall was one of the largest plans for civic development completed in the nation. The mall is used to host a wide variety of public events.

CLEVELAND'S HARBOR. One of Cleveland's major assets has been its location on the southern shore of Lake Erie. At the time this photograph was taken in 1912, the East 9th Street Pier was home for passenger service offered by both the Detroit and Cleveland Navigation Company and the Buffalo and Cleveland Navigation Company. This is a very tranquil scene, perfect for a stroll on the pier.

DOWNTOWN CLEVELAND FROM THE LAKEFRONT. In this aerial view *c.* 1919, the Port of Cleveland is seen, showing the wharves and docks, as well as the rail system that served the lakefront. By 1929, the city's population had surpassed 900,000, while the Greater Cleveland area increased as inner-ring suburbs, particularly on the west side, grew because of the Detroit-Superior High-Level Bridge over the Cuyahoga River, seen on the right.

CLEVELAND'S CROWDED SKYLINE. This 1927 photograph presents a view of downtown Cleveland looking north towards Lake Erie from the Ohio Bell Telephone Company Building located at Prospect Avenue and East 6th Street. Notable landmarks include the Guardian Bank Building on Euclid Avenue, designed by the architectural firm of Walker and Weeks; the Public Auditorium, directly behind the bank; the East 9th Street Pier; and the Cuyahoga County Courthouse.

THE VAN SWERINGEN BROTHERS. It was the vision of businessmen Mantis James (1881–1935) and Oris Paxton (1879–1936) Van Sweringen (left to right) that led to the development of one of Cleveland's most ambitious building projects—the Cleveland Union Terminal Complex on Public Square. Born in poverty, they made their fortune as real estate developers, creating the suburb of Shaker Heights and with it, Shaker Square and the Shaker Rapid.

CHAMPLAIN AVENUE. In order to build the Terminal Tower and a new railroad terminal, entire streets were removed and over 1,400 buildings had to be demolished. In this 1922 photograph, the southeast corner of Champlain Avenue and West 3rd Street is seen. On the corner is the American Telephone and Telegraph Company Building, an interesting structure resembling, in much smaller scale, the Central Armory.

WEST 25TH STREET, WEST SIDE. This is a 1922 photograph of a typical near-west side neighborhood razed for the Terminal Tower Complex at the southwest corner of West 25th Street and Monroe Avenue. The house on the left, 2256, belonged to marble and mosaic artist, Vincent Belfi; the house next door is a residence and storefront for A. Horvath Confectionary and Groceries; and the remaining homes are residential with storefronts.

RIVERBED ROAD. This 1922 photograph shows some of the commercial and residential buildings along the west side of Riverbed Road north of Columbus Road, just before demolition. During the early 19th century, this area west of the Cuyahoga River, east of West 25th Street, and south of Detroit Avenue was populated by Irish immigrants and was known as "Irishtown Bend."

117

THE FOREST CITY HOUSE BLOCK. On the corner of Superior Avenue and Public Square, across the street from the southwest quadrant, stood the Forest City House, which opened in 1852 as one of the oldest and finest hotels in Cleveland. When plans for the Terminal Tower building group were finalized, Forest City House, which closed in 1915, and the rest of the block would be replaced by the Hotel Cleveland.

SOUTH SIDE OF SUPERIOR AVENUE, 1915. An early downtown commercial and business district developed along Superior Avenue between Public Square and the Flats during the 19th century. This 1915 photograph shows the commercial buildings along the south side of Superior Avenue between West 6th Street and the Square, which were torn down for the construction of the Hotel Cleveland, the Cleveland Union Terminal station, and the U.S. Post Office.

THE FOUR CORNERS OF PUBLIC SQUARE. The four quadrants of Public Square are plainly seen in this 1923 aerial view. Across the street from the Hotel Cleveland and across from the recently demolished south side is the southwest quadrant; on the left is the southeast quadrant with the Soldiers and Sailors Monument; at the bottom in the center is the northeast quadrant; and in the bottom right corner is the northwest quadrant.

ST. CLAIR AND ONTARIO AVENUES. This is a 1908 photograph of the southeast corner of St. Clair Avenue and Ontario Avenue, which became the site of the 13-story Engineers Building that housed the Brotherhood of Locomotive Engineers, previously located in the Society for Savings Building. Dedicated in 1910, the Engineers Building cost $1.4 million and was designed by the Cleveland architectural firm of Knox and Elliott.

THE WINTER WONDER OF PUBLIC SQUARE. Cleveland winters can be beautiful, as seen in this 1915 photograph looking east from the southwest corner of Public Square. The southeast corner is decorated with trees, and the whole Square is blanketed by several inches of snow. Superior Avenue can be seen on the left and next to it the Cuyahoga and Williamson Buildings. The May Company is on the right.

THE HIGBEE COMPANY SITE. The businesses and buildings on the southwest corner of Ontario Avenue and Public Square, as seen in this 1920 photograph, are to be razed for the Higbee Company department store, an anchor of the Terminal Tower Complex. Among the storefronts affected were Mays Drug Store, Kendel's Seed Store, Credit to All, and the Hotel Adams. The Higbee Company on Public Square would open for business in 1931.

SOUTH SIDE OF PUBLIC SQUARE, STREET LEVEL. In this 1922 photograph, the commercial block on the south side of Public Square by the southwest quadrant is seen as a hodgepodge of office space and retail storefronts. Included along this block, highlighted atop with advertising for Camel cigarettes and Iodent Toothpaste, are the G.W.S. Mission, the Inter-Urban Station, McKinley Savings and Loan Company, the Niedling Sign Company, and the Square Restaurant.

AERIAL VIEW, SOUTH SIDE OF PUBLIC SQUARE. This is a 1924 photograph of the south side of Public Square, the site of the Terminal Tower and the Higbee Company department store. The building on the right is the Hotel Cleveland, which was built in 1918 and later became the Sheraton Hotel and Stouffer's Inn on the Square. The commercial strip to the left of the hotel included many small stores and office space.

THE MAY COMPANY AND BAILEY'S. Retail competitors Bailey's and the May Company, seen in this photograph of Ontario Avenue, would soon be joined by the Higbee Company department store, which would open across the street following the dedication of the Terminal Tower in 1930. The Bailey Company opened their ten-story building in 1903, followed by a seven-story annex in 1910.

THE HILL STREET GANG. Hill Street once ran south from Central Avenue east of East 9th Street until it was absorbed into the Terminal Tower Complex. In this 1924 photograph, the north side of Hill Street, the 700 block, is seen with a two-story brick apartment building with a street level storefront on the left and the Bailey Company Stables on the right. Our gang of children poses before the camera.

A BIRD'S-EYE VIEW OF PUBLIC SQUARE. This photograph c. 1920 presents a view of the southern half of Public Square, which includes a clear view of Ontario Avenue south of the square. The May Company stores on Euclid Avenue and Prospect Avenue can be seen, along with the Richman Brothers' store on the southeast corner of Ontario and Prospect Avenues. The commercial block under the Weideman sign in the center on the right would be demolished.

VIEW FROM THE FIELD OFFICE. This progress photograph taken in November 1926 presents a view looking south from the field office. Two of Cleveland's major department stores, the May Company on the left and the Bailey Company, or Bailey's, next to it, can be seen on Ontario Avenue. Graham, Anderson, Probst, and White are the architects for the Terminal Tower and Cleveland Union Terminal.

123

A Bird's-Eye View. Taken from the 50th floor of the Terminal Tower, construction workers capture a breathtaking aerial view of Cleveland in August 1927. The view from the yet-to-be-completed observation deck promises to be far and wide. It is hard to imagine that the worker on the left seems at ease with only a slim cable standing between him and disaster.

The Hotel Cleveland. Designed in 1918 by Graham, Burnham, and Company, the Hotel Cleveland on the left remained part of the Terminal Tower building. This photograph taken in June 1927 presents a view looking south from the intersection of Superior Avenue and West 6th Street. The Baltimore and Ohio Railroad station is also to the left of the building. The contractor for the Terminal Tower was John Gill and Sons.

THE OHIO BELL TELEPHONE BUILDING. This is the new 22-story Ohio Bell building as seen from the Terminal Tower on June 1927. It stands 365-feet tall and extends three stories below street level at 700 Prospect Avenue. When completed, this steel framework skyscraper was the tallest building downtown. It was designed by Hubbell and Benes at a cost $5,000,000.

THE VIEW FROM O.B.T. This spectacular photograph was taken in June 1927 from the Ohio Bell Telephone Building and looks westerly toward the Terminal Tower Complex and Cleveland Union Terminal. The steel framework shell of the tower is clearly visible as is Lake Erie, forming a backdrop behind. To the left is the concrete span of the Detroit-Superior High-Level Bridge.

Terminal Tower, 1927. The Cleveland Union Terminal and Terminal Tower were built on the southwest corner of Public Square. In this photograph taken in August, the view is looking west from Ontario Street at the back of the complex. Work remains to be done on the upper floors and at ground level and below, where the subway station is to be built.

The Van Sweringens on the Move. When the brothers O.P. and M.J. Van Sweringen decided to relocate the lakefront railroad depot to Public Square and to build Cleveland Union Terminal and the Terminal Tower Complex, they permanently changed the downtown landscape. For their contribution to Cleveland's development, they were awarded a Medal for Public Service from the Chamber of Commerce. But their empire, however, would collapse during the Great Depression.

TERMINAL TOWER, 1927. Many progress photographs were taken of the historic rise of the Cleveland Union Terminal and the Terminal Tower. This view was taken in October from the Williamson Building and is looking west across Public Square. The complex is nearing completion as only work on the upper floors remains. The Hotel Cleveland can be seen on the right.

CONSTRUCTION WORKERS, 1927. Standing on the observation deck of the Terminal Tower can be challenging for some. Imagine standing on the 50th floor without the benefit of a surrounding deck. These construction workers seem very comfortable standing on the edge and out in the open of Cleveland's tallest structure. The view on this sunny July day must have been spectacular.

SHADOW OF THINGS TO COME. This aerial view of Public Square is taken from the observation deck of the 52-story Terminal Tower as it nears completion in 1928. Looking straight down and across the street from the monument is the Cuyahoga Building at the corner of Superior Avenue. The Soldiers and Sailors Monument, Cleveland's late 19th century landmark located in the southeast quadrant, is now overshadowed by Cleveland's newest landmark. Still standing on the left and anchoring the eastern approach to Euclid Avenue is the taller Williamson Building, partly shadowed by the Terminal Tower's peak. These two buildings would remain for several decades more until progress demanded they be razed.

The Terminal Tower was the pride of the city. A truly great city required an equally great tribute to its industrial and manufacturing strength. The quaint New England-inspired town boasting a Public Square lined with beautiful trees had been replaced by skyscrapers and concrete. On October 23, 1929, the first passenger train entered the Terminal Tower Complex. Six days later, the stock market crashed, ushering in the Great Depression.

Visit us at
arcadiapublishing.com